The Mystery of the X Variable

of the X Variable

by Christopher Williams
illustrated by Julie Olson

HOUGHTON MIFFLIN   BOSTON

Printed in China

ISBN 10: 0-618-89885-9
ISBN 13: 978-0-618-89885-5

14 15 16 17 0940 17 16 15 14 13

4500432010

As students filed into Mr. Chen's classroom, constant chatter filled the air. The excitement was building. Mr. Chen had promised a mystery today. He had told them, "*X* marks the spot," so students were busy looking around the room for the *X*.

After the bell rang, Mr. Chen took attendance. The math warm-up was the first exercise of the day. For this warm-up, Mr. Chen would say some math equations. Students would decide whether each equation was true or false.

"Seven plus—" Mr. Chen began. *TTTTttttt TTTTTtttttTTTT* "—equals twelve," he finished.

The loud sound of a jackhammer just outside the window drowned out part of the math equation. Then there was a knock at the door. Mr. Chen went to the door and was talking to someone in the hall.

Otis whispered to Tu, "I didn't hear what Mr. Chen said. Did you? How can we know if the equation is true when we don't have all the numbers?"

Maria smiled. "Don't worry!" she said. "We can figure out the missing number."

"How?" Tu asked.

Maria walked to the board and wrote:

$$7 + x = 12$$

Then she explained, "We just have to solve for x."

"But how do we solve for x?" a frustrated Asa wanted to know.

Maria said, "Look at the equation. How many do we have in all?"

"12," Asa replied.

Just then, Mr. Chen looked into the room. He saw that the students were busy, so he continued his discussion at the door.

Read·Think·Write Why did Maria use x in her equation?

Maria asked, "What happens if I take away 7 from each side?" She wrote on the board:

$$7 - 7 + x = 12 - 7$$

Then she asked, "How much is 7 minus 7?"

"Zero," Hiro called out.

Maria wrote on the board: $x = 12 - 7$.

"What is 12 minus 7?" she asked.

"Five!" said Percy.

"Now we know that x equals 5," said Maria. "To check the answer, we just substitute 5 for x." She wrote on the board: $7 + 5 = 12$. "Is that equation true or false?" she asked.

"True!" the class shouted.

"Right!" Maria said. "So, if Mr. Chen puts any number but 5 in place of the x, we know the equation is false."

Mr. Chen closed the door. He looked at the board and said, "Nice work. You used a variable to solve the problem. A variable is a letter, such as x, p, or s, that stands for a number."

$$7 + x = 12$$
$$7 - 7 + x = 12 - 7$$
$$x = 5$$
$$7 + 5 = 12$$

"Let's continue," said Mr. Chen. *BEEP…BEEP… BEEP* "—minus 7 equals 12."

"Six multiplied by—" *ZZZZZZZZzzzzzzzz* "—equals 48."

THUNK…THUNK "—divided by 9 equals 8."

Students' hands were shooting into the air when there was another knock at the door. Mr. Chen went to answer. The students all looked at Maria.

Maria quickly stepped to the front of the room and said, "We can use *x* again to help us solve these equations." She wrote the equations on the board.

Read·Think·Write What does *6x* mean?

"Here are the equations. I put x in the place of the numbers we couldn't hear. Now we just need to solve for x," Maria said. "And remember, what you do to one side of an equation you must do to the other side."

Ava quickly solved for x in $x - 7 = 12$. She added 7 to each side of the equation, $x - 7 + 7 = 12 + 7$.

"That was easy!" she said. "$x = 19$."

Hoon was solving for x in $6x = 48$. "I divide both sides by 6. So, $x = 8$."

Ava and Hoon watched Ella solving for x in $x \div 9 = 8$. She multiplied 9×8.

"72," Ava, Hoon, and Ella said together.

Everyone checked their answers and found that they had correctly solved for x.

Ava's work	Hoon's work	Ella's work
$x - 7 = 12$	$6x = 48$	$x \div 9 = 8$
$x - 7 + 7 = 12 + 7$	$6x \div 6 = 48 \div 6$	$x \div 9 \times 9 = 8 \times 9$
$x = 19$	$x = 8$	$x = 72$
$19 - 7 = 12$	$6 \times 8 = 48$	$72 \div 9 = 8$

Read·Think·Write How do the students check their answers?

Mr. Chen was smiling as he said, "Well, class, it looks like you figured out today's mystery without me."

Tao said, "I thought x marked the spot for buried treasure. But now I see that x marks the spot for a number. All I have to do is solve for it."

"That's right, Tao," Mr. Chen said. "Knowing how to solve for x unlocks lots of secrets. We'll talk more about that in a bit. First, gather up your books. My visitor has found us a quieter room, so you can hear me and my words won't be a mystery."

The class laughed. The morning had been full of mystery, just as Mr. Chen had promised.

1. What is a variable in an equation?

2. What does x stand for in the equation $6x = 24$?

3. How did you solve for x in question 2?

4. How can you check to see if the answer to question 2 is correct?

Activity

Note Important Details Use two-sided counters as needed to help solve this number story. Max has 20 crayons. He has 5 more crayons than Emily. How many crayons does Emily have? Use a variable to help you write a number sentence to find the answer.